Josef Tomáš, born in Czechoslovakia in 1933, pursued a mechanical engineering degree at the Czech Technical University in Prague, graduating in 1957. His academic journey continued with a PhD in the Theory of Nonlinear Vibrations from the Czech Academy of Sciences in 1966. Until 1993, he held a professorship, later transitioning to the role of owner and director of Advea, an engineering company in Melbourne, until his retirement in 2010

He wrote his first poems in 1980 in the form of letters to his mother. He underwent an intensive learning period from 1980 to 1986, following the advice of T.S. Eliot: "Who wishes to write poetry must keep in training and must do this by good workmanship for some hours' work every week of his life." During this period he wrote over 500 poems, mostly on the train from Glen Waverley to the City and back. He then wrote poetry in English under the guidance of Australian poet Philip Martin from 1986 to 1989.

A prolific author, Tomáš has penned ten books of poetry in Czech and, since 2006, has translated the works of many Czech poets, along with two of his own books, into English.

This collection is dedicated to the memory of the late Philip Martin.

Josef A Tomáš

SIMPLE EXERCISES

AUSTIN MACAULEY PUBLISHERS™
LONDON • CAMBRIDGE • NEW YORK • SHARJAH

Copyright © Josef A Tomáš 2024

The right of Josef A Tomáš to be identified as author of this work has been asserted by the author in accordance with sections 77 and 78 of the Copyright, Designs and Patents Act 1988.

All rights reserved. No part of this publication may be reproduced, stored in a retrieval system, or transmitted in any form or by any means, electronic, mechanical, photocopying, recording, or otherwise, without the prior permission of the publishers.

Any person who commits any unauthorised act in relation to this publication may be liable to criminal prosecution and civil claims for damages.

A CIP catalogue record for this title is available from the British Library.

ISBN 9781035810161 (Paperback)
ISBN 9781035810178 (ePub e-book)

www.austinmacauley.com

First Published 2024
Austin Macauley Publishers Ltd®
1 Canada Square
Canary Wharf
London
E14 5AA

Thanks to poet Adham Smart for his assistance with the publication of this book.

Table of Contents

My Poems in English	11
On the Morning Train	13
Sunday Morning	14
Restaurant by the Sea	15
Last Day of Holidays	16
A Quiet Hour	17
Post Meridiem	18
Self-Portrait	19
A Cut	20
A Cold Day	21
A Cup of Tea	22
Return from School	23
They Died Just Below the Summit	24
Light	26
Now	27
I Found You, God!	28
Soprano	29
After a Party	30
How a Diamond Feels	31

Wheelers Hill	32
Men Everywhere	33
View from Museum Station	34
Changing Trains at Richmond	35
A Little Girl	36
View from Syndal Station	37
Collins Street	38
Melbourne, Late Autumn	39
There Is No Reason	40
Shoes	41
Dreaming Fishermen	42
Fauré's Requiem	43

My Poems in English

These poems date from a transitional period between 1986 and 1989 when, after my mother's death in 1986, I stopped writing in Czech until 1995. I was encouraged to write in English by the late Australian poet Professor Philip Martin. In 1983, I saw a film which went behind the scenes of the conductor Sergiu Celibidache rehearsing Fauré's Requiem with the London Symphony Orchestra. I used to play bridge with a lady who studied English and creative writing with Philip, and she knew that I wrote poetry in Czech. I translated my poem *Fauré's Requiem* into English for her and told her about my fascination with Celibidache. This sparked her interest because she knew that her professor also admired Celibidache very much, and had written about the same Requiem in 1984.

A few days later, she arranged a dinner with Philip. He brought with him a copy of his essay and poem, and also gave me a video of that rehearsal which had captivated us both so much. We talked about my poetry; he wondered why I was writing in Czech at all when the communist regime in my home country would not allow any work by a political refugee to be published, and suggested I begin writing in English. I cannot overstate Philip's importance to my growth as a writer and translator.

The poems are inspired mainly by everyday experiences on the train journey from Glen Waverley to Melbourne city centre and back, as well as by the city of Melbourne itself. Were it not for this daily travel routine, I would have written very little during this period. Apart from the train experience, the poems speak mainly of the sea, because to this day, the sea has remained something extraordinary for me, as though 42 years spent in the very interior of Europe had starved me of open space in some strange way.

On the Morning Train

Looks. Thoughtful. Serious.
Some still in sleep,
with half-closed eyes echoing
short-lived night-time pleasures.

Men. Not talking. Inside selves.
Floating like logs, soaked with dreams,
beneath the undulating chatter
of boisterous schoolchildren.

Souls. Content and happy
in quiet compartments
below switched-off brains.
Not quite prepared yet
to fill the empty tanks of their minds
with the corrosives of another day.

Sunday Morning

Sunday morning is drenched in the peace
which our sleep garnered overnight,
having suddenly no need to worry
about the straitjackets of monotony,
which restrain us throughout the week.

Sunday morning bathes us in peace.
Orders, prescriptions, duties, plans
are locked in attaché cases,
lazing in the same dark places,
they were left on Friday night.

Sunday morning plays with peace.
Every adult is keen to join
a dream-game to discover where
his mother, now forever gone,
might have hidden his favourite toy.

Restaurant by the Sea

The windows are cut in half
by the horizon of the sea;
landscapes hung on walls,
in a restaurant where bodies
are fed more through the eyes
than through hungry throats.

White clouds crowning the windows
hang above blue waters, blanched
here and there by waves, or
the sails of miniature boats.

A still-life of scallops, crabs and fish
getting cold on silver plates;
waiting in open coffins
for the ocean to come and deliver
a chomping speech at their funeral.

Last Day of Holidays

What god-like idleness
rests in the self-satisfied hands
of the evening before the next
long spell of work!

No looking-in-advance disturbs,
no remembering penetrates
the distended walls of swollen boredom.

A secret mixture
of warming earth and cooling air
bribes the senses to accept and savour
the idleness of god-like holidays.

A Quiet Hour

A quiet hour. A lake
behind a closed weir
on a river. A time
to recall how much
I've already seen
above raised banks…

To restart a dream
of new fields and towns
along the hurrying stream,
postponing the thought
of how close already
the waiting sea might be…

Yet to notice well the greater
width and depth of the riverbed,
supplied and fed by water
from so many brooks and tears
that I cannot distinguish
what is mine, and what I owe.

Post Meridiem

An afternoon of cosy togetherness
inside a warm, dry house,
while the rain and wind take over outside,
tearing the green woollen shield
off the fresh aquarelles of walls and roofs.

An afternoon of unexpected looks
through a greasy web of "already seen"
and "already heard many times before"
falling through smiles, through eyes,
focused on the infinity of life.

An afternoon of hesitation,
motionless behind vibrating words,
so patient, with ever-changing aims,
as if already tidying and washing up
the cups and saucers of our emptied minds.

An afternoon of contemplation.

Self-Portrait

I am the man who knows
very little. The man who enjoys
playing game after game
when loss and victory
have lost any meaning.

I am the man who tries
very little. The man who prefers
watching to doing
when gain and failure
have lost any meaning.

I am the man who believes
in very little. The man who sees
with his heart rather than his brain
when thoughts and words cannot replace
the art of unadulterated sight.

A Cut

A cut through impervious time,
achieved by forgetting
the incoming hours and days
to concentrate solely
on the wondrous present.

A cut, a wedge that,
like lightning,
splits each of us apart
to expose the heartwood
of a forgotten past.

A cut, deep through the toughness
of stockpiled thoughts,
as by a craftsman's chisel
or a surgeon's knife,
seeking the knot of truth.

A cut to bloodlet dreams,
futile, rotten memories,
as by a barber's razor,
rejuvenating in us
never-aging life.

A Cold Day

It was so cold
that even the light
lost its colour, and space
reflected only
what was evident anyway.

Everyone's limbs were cold,
and the steam of their breath
disappeared
just after it was exhaled.

The Earth has tilted
towards one of its poles
to show us
what death really means:
absolute zero,
endless emptiness.

A Cup of Tea

Water poured on dry leaves
in a mindless act
of creation. A new existence,
a cup-of-tea, appears from nowhere
and (for a little while) lives.
Then a few gulps of a thirsty man
will finish it forever.
An empty pot will remain,
and a warming feeling,
sinking down and disappearing
inside a hollow body.

Return from School

Children are coming home from school.
The moon, on the wall of the railway station
has always been here. The train will come soon,

as it does every day, to take them for a ride
right through the country that they know well.
They quickly forget what they leave behind

in their classrooms filled with abstract things.
The wings of their fantasies flapping away,
not thinking about what the next day brings.

To them, the adult world is strange.
Plans and duties, the repetition of tasks
are closed books for another age.

They see things from a rainbow point of view,
beauty in the pictures they paint of their world,
not yet afraid to start each day anew.

They Died Just Below the Summit

They died just below the summit
of Mount Everest. One of them
was my neighbour's son.
His father's petrified look
was abrupt emptiness
after the news arrived,
his mother's face soft
with tears under terrified eyes.

Why was I unable to hide a smile?
I was dumbfounded by an innermost voice,
whispering to me that one could not find
a better death than on the slopes
of the Tibetan side of Chomolungma,
where everybody has faith
in the transmigration of souls,
the blissful peace of Nirvana.

If Buddha turns out to be right,
then it did not happen much.
Two Selves returned to their Source;
maybe earlier than some of us,
but much later than many others.
One day, we shall remember them again
at the white foothills
of sweaty hospital blankets.

Light

Light through the window.
A dispersed Sun.
Golden arrows shatter
on the armour of air.
A devastating war
shifting easily
into a silent peace…
An angel in a thin white robe
descended on the lonely Earth,
to make grass green and roses red,
and fill up a few human hearts
with joy and love.

Now

Now… merely a word, and yet
it takes off like an aeroplane
for a voyage around the world.

Now… really here and rising,
like a dust storm which later falls
and covers all past and future lands.

Now… an inert projectile,
fired long ago, but still flying
towards a forgotten goal.

Now… silencing futile dreams
with the ubiquity of its sounds,
born from the nothingness of "N".

Now… showing its full beauty,
after the doubtful "double-yous" capsized,
unshackling the sacred word "Om".

I Found You, God!

I found you, God, finally I did,
hidden so well and for so long
behind dead things and living faces,
letting me search for you so blindly
in the impossible reaches of the universe.

Now I know precisely where you are:
not there in front of me, but as if behind
the corner of a moving screen,
or the veil of a lovely wife, afraid
that her beauty might dazzle my eyes.

You are everywhere – but not in the open,
changing bodies and stems and leaves
like handkerchiefs or vests or suits;
as if your need for us were at least
as great as ours is for you.

Soprano

The air, the breath,
forced suddenly out of her chest
by the gentle urges of her mind,
will not sing on their own.
It must have taken days to memorise the tune,
and many years of hard work to acquire
the skills to automate the opening and closing
of concealed pipes inside her slender throat.
She sings with such ease,
as if it were a simple exercise
to resonate the invisible gas,
which fills completely the voluminous hall
with its dissolved mass.
But she knows how to move it fore and aft
with the gentle force of her trembling lungs
according to her strong-willed mind,
and how to soften our hardened hearts
with a three-hundred-year-old song.

After a Party

The guests are gone.
The lamp hangs high
above the tablecloth
so as not to get in the way
when the empty plates and glasses
are being put away.

The room is vacant
of smiles and words.
Fingerprints only
and the impressions of lips
on the rims of glasses
betray the sudden silence.

Not for long.
Carried away and washed,
they, too, are put aside
to lie as if paralysed
by an intrusive thought
about how little has remained
from what seemed so much
just a little while ago.

How a Diamond Feels

At least twice a day,
I get to feel
the toughness of life.
When I drive my car
over a narrow ditch
of concealed earth
and across a concrete bridge,
I feel my cemented self
(which started fluid and soft
so many years ago)
harden more and more.

Today, I feel like a diamond,
only instead of glass
I cut the minds of others.

Wheelers Hill

Gables and ridges
piled up above trees
are concealing
a suburban hill.

They remind me
of cut-price dresses
in the supermarket
hidden on the right.

No men are seen,
no smoke rises up
from chimneyless roofs;
no lights in windows
to welcome the dawn.

Only a few lamps
hover over streets
like half-deflated
air balloons, forgotten
from yesterday's fete.

Men Everywhere

Like a sea with waves of words and deeds,
sometimes crashing over me,
yet other times quite gently touching
my overloaded senses.

Like a drop of water, I am
evaporating towards mysterious clouds,
leaving only hard layers of stone
all over the bottom and around the sides
of the cooking pot of the world.

Later, purified, I come down as rain
to clean and cool the busy foreheads.
At last, there is no need for theatrics,
no place for intoxicating words.

View from Museum Station

Loose stones and bricks are stacked
in cubicle piles of houses,
held together by glass
and concrete skins and iron spines.
A maze of oversized steps helps
emerging shadows to climb up
from darkened streets and chase
the mirages of invisible suns.

No tree, no man; just immovable matter,
piled up over one mile squared;
not a trace of weathered earth
with even the tiniest hope for life.
The soil left years ago;
bare clay and naked rock encased
in concrete armour metres deep,
compressed yet deeper by its own weight.

No trees, no men in view;
only the last reflections of a reddish sun,
swallowed by the darkness from below.
Then night-time's silent aeroplanes
start landing one after the other
on the evacuated town.

Changing Trains at Richmond

The seat is still full
of vibrating molecules,
excited by the warmth
of a living body.

Modulated by thoughts
and dreams and feelings,
it keeps warm while waiting
for my living body.

If I come late, the cold
will silence it all,
as the cold will do
to any living body.

A Little Girl

To Kathy

Speech arises out of me
like water from a spring.
Water gushing over the stones
of the big people around me
falls into the valley of my dreams.

I'm nestled up on both sides of myself.
I'm stirring up, all around,
the stagnant water of life,
with my hands, my eyes, my whole body.

On the shores of my being,
I sing to myself,
not knowing that in the eyes of some
the flowers of my words
have just now been set in motion.

View from Syndal Station

Sleep must have been good tonight
in the woolly bed of leaves;
the houses are waiting quietly
for the belated sun.

The tilted foreheads of houses
rest on grey-green pillows,
windows closed tight
beneath pondering trees.

Dreams of houses. Working every night
in foreign countries with strange men;
working so hard, yet always bringing
hardly anything back.

People, who dream in these houses,
get up and eat and dress,
the same every single morning:
a short walk and they forget

all about the night. Only their eyes
hint at unknown depths,
just before another ordinary day
closes them firmly.

Collins Street

The net of branches is full of holes,
reminding us that autumn has indeed
ended. The day is sunny but not warm.
People wear long coats, or at least
pullovers in dull colours, and walk slowly
as if boasting about all their spare time.

The pointed tower
of an old church is
an outstretched hand,
reaching for heaven,
where only patches of sky
hang above soaring walls.

Melbourne, Late Autumn

The day is windy, but this year
autumn has been kind to us,
the weather beautiful and warm
till the middle of May.
At home, these would have been
the months of falling leaves…

Today, I've seen them falling
even in this town of inert eucalypts;
scarcely, and yet falling still
from imported trees planted
around the green playgrounds
in strange oval shapes. For a moment,
I almost feel at home.

Dead leaves jumping like a flock of fleas
on the skin of a neglected dog. After all,
who really cares for the naked earth,
to let her face the incoming winter
without even a blanket of snow?

There Is No Reason

You, my love, who are
no longer here,
there is no reason
to be sad. After all,
to meet always meant
to part. So what sense
does it make to keep
repeating?

If you pierce through
all your layers,
you'll find that I was
with you long before
we met… So why
continue pretending
that there was ever
something to be lost?

Shoes

Apart. As if just left
by a pair of feet;
taken by surprise
and not believing yet
that it may be
for a long time, or for good.

Deserted islands,
missing so much
the long leg of Italy
when all the summer guests have left
for their cold homes
far in the north of Europe.

They still hope that one day,
somebody will feel
abandoned like they,
and will cover the curves
of their bare insoles
with tender-hearted looks.

Dreaming Fishermen

There is no aim in me anymore.
Quiet are my days, one by one
the same and bobbing
like the corks of dreaming fishermen,
who forget completely how they got here.

They sit on the railings of a bridge,
surprised by the ease with which
they balance the emptiness
that always threatened them
from below their lives.

Their eyes are closed, their lids
are motionless, their faces
so peaceful and so thin,
that the Infinite can surely
walk through them as it pleases.

Fauré's Requiem

As if all that can hover
embarked upon rising
up and towards heaven.
All that detached itself
from everyday haste
which has no end, which has no end.

It is not the soul of the deceased one,
who, only a few hours ago,
was moving and talking to us,
as we were to him, and as we
still talk to one another now.

It is not the soul of the dead one;
that was detached by dying,
opposing and resisting at first,
unsure what to do,
suddenly, without the corpse.

It is our transformed selves,
ourselves after amazement.
The selves that could not believe
that fear might really be
the last thing that would remain,
and, therefore, they dared

to turn back and to go,
steadily and stubbornly, inside themselves,
so long as all that ties and binds
does not dissolve into nothing.

Now, they hover and slowly rise,
and feel how they draw near
to the God inside them.

Made in the USA
Monee, IL
03 May 2026